World Cultures
AND
GEOGRAPHY

Workbook

McDougal Littell
Evanston, Illinois • Boston • Dallas

Printed in the United States of America

ISBN 0-618-19921-7

5 6 7 8 9 -MDO- 06 05 04

Contents

Guided Reading

A. Taking Notes As you read this section, find facts about the five fields of learning that are part of social studies. Write them in the chart below.

Fields of Learning	Facts
History	
Geography	
Government	
Economics	
Culture	

B. Summarizing On the back of this paper, identify or explain each of the following:

social studies   unlimited government   market economy

Guided Reading

A. Identifying Main Ideas As you read, take notes on aspects of their lives that people in a culture region may have in common.

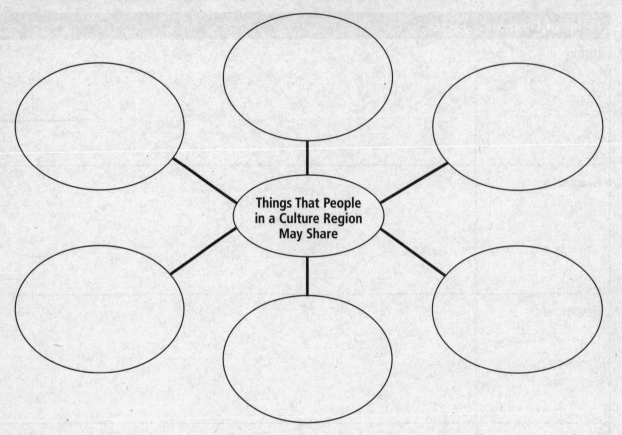

Things That People
in a Culture Region
May Share

B. Summarizing On the back of this paper, give some examples that show how the United States is a multicultural society.

Guided Reading

A. Taking Notes As you read this section, take notes about geography's five themes.

Theme	Notes
Location	
Place	
Region	
Movement	
Human-Environment Interaction	

B. Summarizing On the back of this paper, briefly discuss how and why people move from one place to another. Include an explanation of the term *push and pull factors*. Describe physical features that may make migration easy or difficult.

Guided Reading

A. Taking Notes As you read this section, take notes about the topics shown in the chart below.

Maps and Globes	
Comparing Maps and Globes	
Three Kinds of Maps	
Map Projections	

B. Summarizing On the back of this paper, explain why graphs are useful tools for geographers.

Guided Reading

A. Comparing Use this Venn diagram to compare and contrast the
Intermountain Region and the Atlantic Coastal Plain.

Intermountain Region **Common Features** **Atlantic Coastal Plain**

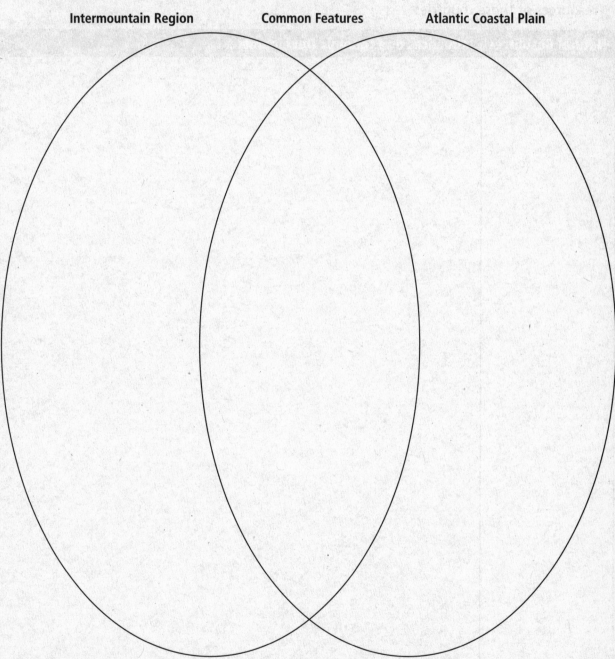

B. Summarizing On the back of this paper, explain what a landform is.
Then describe how glaciers and erosion contribute to the formation
of landforms.

Guided Reading

A. Drawing Conclusions Use this chart to show how the economic development of the United States and Canada is influenced by the natural resources of those countries.

Natural Resources	Influences on Economic Development

B. Summarizing On the back of this paper, explain the difference between climate and weather.

Guided Reading

A. Finding Main Ideas As you read this section, use this chart to take notes about different groups who moved to America.

Groups	Notes

B. Summarizing On the back of this paper, explain the rights and responsibilities that citizens have in the United States.

Guided Reading

A. Taking Notes Use this chart to take notes about the three branches of the U.S. federal government.

Three Branches of Government	Notes

B. Summarizing On the back of this paper, explain what the U.S. Constitution is and why it was written.

Guided Reading

A. Finding Main Ideas Use this chart to take notes about the United States economy.

Notes
Goods and Services
Factors of Production
Free Enterprise/ Market Economy
Supply and Demand

B. Summarizing On the back of this paper, explain the difference between a command economy and a traditional economy.

CHAPTER
4

Section 4 (pages 110–113)

Guided Reading

A. Taking Notes As you read this section, take notes on American culture.

	Examples	Influences
American Values		
Arts and Entertainment		

B. Summarizing On the back of this paper, explain what factors allowed discoveries made by U.S. scientists to reach people around the world.

Name _____ Date _____

Guided Reading

A. Finding Main Ideas Use this chart to take notes about people who have settled in Canada.

Canadians			
Canadian People: Overview	First Nations	European Immigrants	Recent Immigrants

B. Making Inferences On the back of this paper, answer the following question: Why might Canada's policy of multiculturalism make Canada appealing to immigrants?

Guided Reading

A. Categorizing In the boxes below, briefly describe Canada's government.

Constitutional Monarchy

Legislature

Judiciary

B. Summarizing On the back of this sheet of paper, explain the importance to Canada of the Charter of Rights and Freedoms.

Guided Reading

A. Taking Notes Use this chart to take notes about Canada's economy.

Contributors to Canada's Economy		
Natural Resources	**Trade**	**Types of Industries**

B. Contrasting On the back of this paper, explain the difference between transportation corridors and transportation barriers.

Guided Reading

A. Taking Notes Use this chart to record different aspects of Canada's culture.

Canadian Culture	
Languages	
Arts and Entertainment	
Religion	
Culture Regions	

B. Summarizing On the back of this paper, explain why Canadians seek a national identity.

Guided Reading

A. Categorizing As you read this section, use the chart below to categorize information on the geography of Latin America.

Geography of Latin America			
	Boundaries or Location	Characteristics of the Landscape	Volcanic Activity and Earthquakes
Mexico			
Central America			
Caribbean Islands			
South America			

B. Summarizing On the back of this paper, identify or explain each of the following:

deforestation   **Tropical Zone**   *El Niño*

Guided Reading

A. Comparing Use the chart below to take notes that will help you compare the three major civilizations of ancient Latin America.

	Maya	Aztec	Inca
Lands Ruled			
Agricultural Methods			
Intellectual Advances			
Reasons for Decline			

B. Summarizing On the back of this paper, identify or explain each of the following:

Hernán Cortés   **Francisco Pizarro**   **Columbian Exchange**

Guided Reading

A. Finding Main Ideas As you read this section, answer the questions next to the time line.

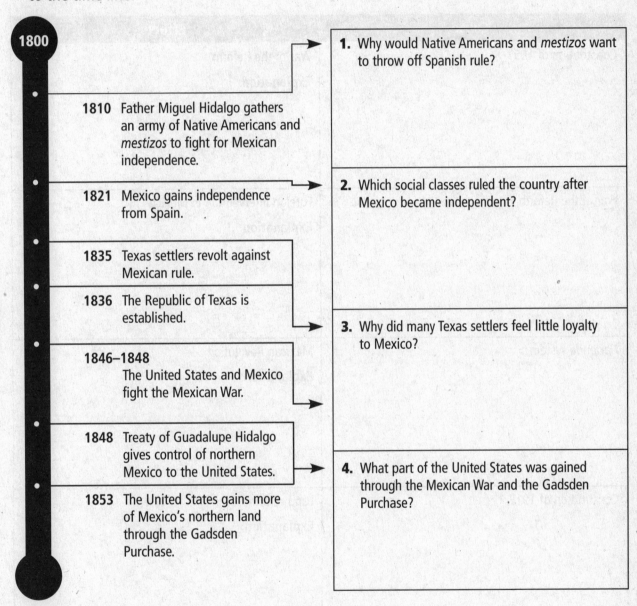

1800

1810 Father Miguel Hidalgo gathers an army of Native Americans and *mestizos* to fight for Mexican independence.

1821 Mexico gains independence from Spain.

1835 Texas settlers revolt against Mexican rule.

1836 The Republic of Texas is established.

1846–1848 The United States and Mexico fight the Mexican War.

1848 Treaty of Guadalupe Hidalgo gives control of northern Mexico to the United States.

1853 The United States gains more of Mexico's northern land through the Gadsden Purchase.

1. Why would Native Americans and *mestizos* want to throw off Spanish rule?

2. Which social classes ruled the country after Mexico became independent?

3. Why did many Texas settlers feel little loyalty to Mexico?

4. What part of the United States was gained through the Mexican War and the Gadsden Purchase?

B. Summarizing On the back of this paper, identify or explain each of the following:

Montezuma   Tenochtitlán   New Spain

Guided Reading

A. Recognizing Effects As you read this section, take notes explaining how the causes below might have helped bring about the effects shown.

Cause	Effects
Constitution of 1857	War of the Reform **Explanation:**
War of the Reform	Foreign intervention in Mexico **Explanation:**
Hacienda system	Mexican Revolution **Explanation:**
Constitution of 1917	Land reform **Explanation:**

B. Summarizing On the back of this paper, identify or explain each of the following:

   Benito Juárez   **Mexican Revolution**   **Institutional Revolutionary Party**

Name _____ Date _____

Guided Reading

A. Categorizing As you read, use the chart below to categorize information in the section on the economy of modern Mexico.

Privatization of Agriculture	Privatization of Business	Foreign Investment in Mexico	Tourism

B. Summarizing On the back of this paper, identify or explain each of the following:

ejido system   *maquiladora*   **PEMEX**

Guided Reading

A. Taking Notes As you read this section, use the chart below to take notes on aspects of Mexican culture.

	Notes
Art and Artists	
City Life	
Country Life	
Holidays	

B. Summarizing On the back of this paper, identify or define each of the following:

Diego Rivera **Plaza of Three Cultures** **Day of the Dead**

Guided Reading

A. Finding Main Ideas As you read this section, use the chart below to help you answer questions about the different ethnic groups in the Caribbean Islands and Central America.

	Central America	Caribbean Islands
Native Americans What happened to local Native Americans after the Spanish arrived?		
Africans How and why were Africans brought to the region?		
Colonists Who colonized the region?		
Ethnic Groups What ethnic backgrounds are mixed in the people of the region today? What are these people called?		

B. Summarizing On the back of this paper, identify or explain each of the following:

    Central America   **dependency**   **Panama Canal**

Guided Reading

A. Taking Notes Fill out the chart below as you read about the economy
of the Caribbean Islands.

Colonial Period
1. What part did the sugar industry play in the Caribbean economy during the colonial period?

Slavery
2. How was slavery important in the Caribbean economy?

Diversification
3. Why did relying on a single product make the Caribbean economy unstable? How did islanders try to make their economy more stable?

B Summarizing As you read about the economy and culture of Central
America, summarize information on the following topics.

Economy Coffee Bananas Other Industries	
Culture Languages Religions	

Section 3 (pages 215–220)

Workbook

Guided Reading

A. Sequencing Events As you read this section on modern Cuba, answer the questions next to the time line.

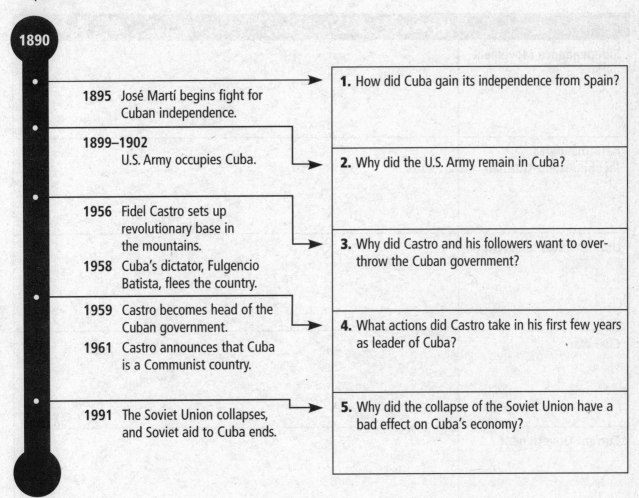

1890

1895 José Martí begins fight for Cuban independence.

1899–1902 U.S. Army occupies Cuba.

1956 Fidel Castro sets up revolutionary base in the mountains.

1958 Cuba's dictator, Fulgencio Batista, flees the country.

1959 Castro becomes head of the Cuban government.

1961 Castro announces that Cuba is a Communist country.

1991 The Soviet Union collapses, and Soviet aid to Cuba ends.

1. How did Cuba gain its independence from Spain?

2. Why did the U.S. Army remain in Cuba?

3. Why did Castro and his followers want to overthrow the Cuban government?

4. What actions did Castro take in his first few years as leader of Cuba?

5. Why did the collapse of the Soviet Union have a bad effect on Cuba's economy?

B. Summarizing On the back of this paper, identify or explain how each of the following has affected Cuba:

Cold War   sugar cane   malnutrition

Name _____ Date _____

Guided Reading

A. Categorizing As you read this section, use the chart to take notes on Guatemalan history and life.

	Notes
Independence Movement	
Reforms under Jacobo Arbenz Guzmán	
United States Intervention	
Civil War	
Current Government	
Economy Today	

B. Summarizing On the back of this paper, identify or explain each of the following as it relates to Guatemala:

United Fruit Company   CIA   Maya people

Guided Reading

A. Identifying Main Ideas As you read this section, write down the main idea of the text under each heading.

Heading	Main Ideas
Europeans Arrive in South America	
Independence	
Governments of South America	
The People of South America	

B. Summarizing On the back of this paper, tell what each of the following people accomplished:

Simón Bolívar   José de San Martín

Guided Reading

A. Contrasting As you read this section, write down the strengths and weaknesses of South American economies.

South American Economies	
Strengths	**Weaknesses**

B. Summarizing On the back of this paper, explain what *urbanization* is and how it has affected South America.

Guided Reading

A. Making Generalizations As you read this section, write down one accurate generalization about each part of Brazil. Use complete sentences.

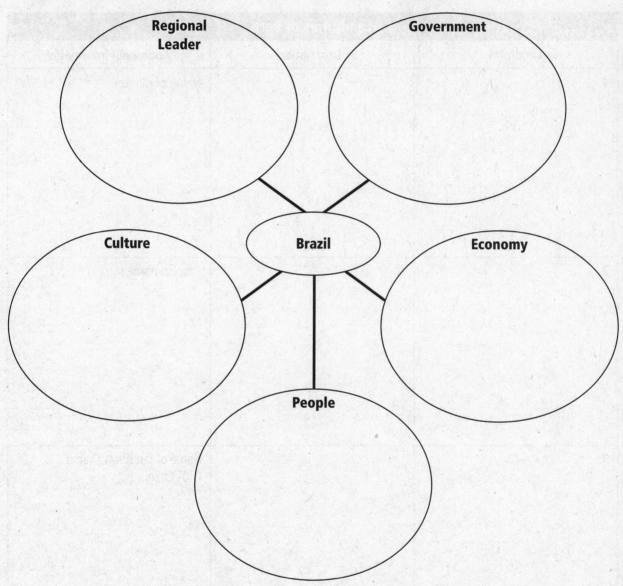

Regional Leader

Government

Culture

Brazil

Economy

People

B. Summarizing On the back of this paper, explain why Brazil's people and culture can be called diverse, or varied.

Guided Reading

A. Categorizing As you read this section, complete the chart about the land of Peru.

Landforms of Peru		
Landform	Description	Additional Information
1.		Name of range:
2.		Spanish name for:
3.		Name of landform shared with Chile:

B. Summarizing On the back of this paper, write one sentence about each of the topics below.

mining in Peru   Sendero Luminoso   Lima

Guided Reading

A. Taking Notes As you read this section, take notes on the following topics.

	Notes
Geographic Features of Europe	
Europe's Climate	
Natural Resources of Europe	

B. Summarizing On the back of this paper, identify or explain each of the following:

    Gulf Stream   **Iberian Peninsula**   **Scandinavian Peninsula**   **Great European Plain**

Guided Reading

A. Recognizing Effects Fill in the chart as you read this section. Note how each accomplishment affected ancient Greek civilization.

Accomplishment	Effects
1. Formation of city-states	
2. Growth of colonies	
3. Development of Greek literature	
4. Birth of Greek philosophy	

B. Forming and Supporting Opinions Fill in the chart below. In the left-hand box, state whether you approve or disapprove of Sparta's required military training. In the right-hand box, list two reasons to support your opinion.

Your Opinion of Sparta's Required Military Training	Supporting Reasons
	1. **2.**

CHAPTER 10

Section 3 (pages 284–289)

Guided Reading

A. Finding Main Ideas As you read this section, answer the questions next to the time line.

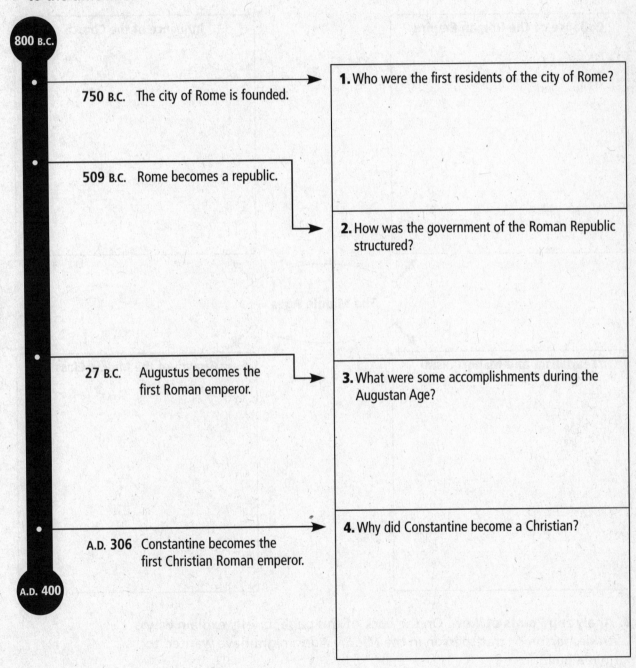

800 B.C.

750 B.C. The city of Rome is founded.

1. Who were the first residents of the city of Rome?

509 B.C. Rome becomes a republic.

2. How was the government of the Roman Republic structured?

27 B.C. Augustus becomes the first Roman emperor.

3. What were some accomplishments during the Augustan Age?

A.D. 306 Constantine becomes the first Christian Roman emperor.

4. Why did Constantine become a Christian?

A.D. 400

B. Summarizing On the back of this paper, identify or explain each of the following:

Pax Romana   **Law of the Twelve Tables**   *mare nostrum*   **aqueduct**

Guided Reading

A. Taking Notes As you read this section, fill in the diagram below with notes about the Middle Ages.

Collapse of the Roman Empire	Influence of the Church

The Middle Ages

Feudalism and Manorialism	Growth of the Middle Class

B. Analyzing Points of View On the back of this page, briefly explain why a tradesperson or craftsperson in the Middle Ages might have wanted to join a guild.

Name _____ Date _____

CHAPTER 11

Guided Reading

A. Taking Notes As you read this section, take notes on the following topics.

	Notes
The Crusades	
The Renaissance in Italy	
Renaissance Art	
The Northern Renaissance	
The Reformation	
Protestantism	

B. Summarizing On the back of this paper, identify or explain each of the following:

patrons   **Leonardo da Vinci**   **Counter Reformation**

Guided Reading

A. Taking Notes As you read this section, take notes on the following topics.

	Notes
The Spice Trade in Europe	
Exploration	
Clash of Cultures	

B. Summarizing To summarize what you have learned about the European explorers, answer the questions below.

Explorer	Nationality?	In what direction did he sail?	Final outcome of expedition?
Bartolomeu Dias			
Vasco da Gama			
Christopher Columbus			
Ferdinand Magellan			
John Cabot			

Name _____ Date _____

Guided Reading

A. Recognizing Effects As you read this section, write notes about the effects of the Scientific and Industrial Revolutions.

Development	Effects
New inventions in science	
Use of steam power	
Growth of cities	
Textile factories in England	
Spread of industrialization	

B. Summarizing On the back of this paper, identify or explain each of the following:

the Bastille   the French Republic   Napoleon Bonaparte

Guided Reading

A. Categorizing As you read, take notes about the Russian czars discussed in the section.

1. Ivan the Terrible	**2.** Peter the Great
3. Catherine the Great	**4.** Nicholas II

B. Finding Main Ideas On the back of this paper, identify or explain the following:

Mongols   **serfs**   **Bloody Sunday**

Guided Reading

A. Finding Main Ideas As you read the section, fill in the cluster diagrams with details that answer the questions.

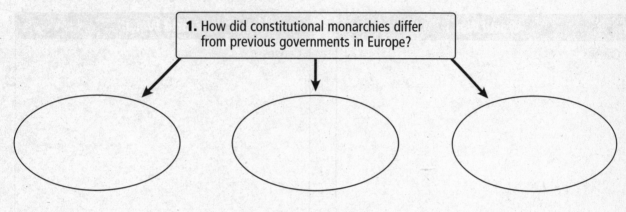

1. How did constitutional monarchies differ from previous governments in Europe?

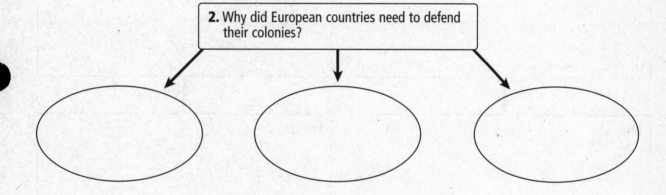

2. Why did European countries need to defend their colonies?

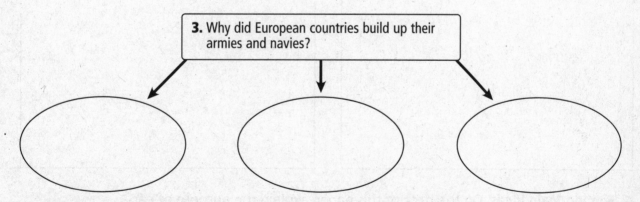

3. Why did European countries build up their armies and navies?

B. Recognizing Effects On the back of this paper, explain how the right to vote led to the development of constitutional monarchies in Europe.

Guided Reading

A. Recognizing Causes and Effects As you read the section, write in the diagrams the causes and effects of World Wars I and II.

World War I
Causes

↓

Effects

World War II
Causes

↓

Effects

B. Finding Main Ideas On the back of this paper, explain the purpose of each of the following:

the Treaty of Versailles   the Marshall Plan

Guided Reading

A. Finding Main Ideas As you read this section, fill out the chart below on the Soviet Union after World War II.

Issue	Main Idea	Details
The Iron Curtain		
Soviet Control of Eastern Europe		
Joseph Stalin's Rule		
Soviet Industry and Agriculture		
The Cold War		

B. Summarizing On the back of this paper, explain how the Soviet Union became so powerful after World War II.

CHAPTER 13

Guided Reading

A. Summarizing As you read, use the chart below to summarize the information in the section on Eastern Europe under communism.

Soviet Culture and Economy	Attempts at Change
National identity	Khrushchev
Daily life	Prague Spring
Literature and the arts	Détente
Sports	Economic crisis (1980s)

B. Comparing On the back of this page, write a paragraph comparing these two leaders:

Nikita Khrushchev   Alexander Dubček

Guided Reading

A. Categorizing As you read, use the chart below to categorize the information in the section on Eastern Europe and Russia.

	Government	Economy	Culture
Eastern Europe			
Russia			

B. Sequencing Events Label the time line below to show the sequence of events discussed in the section.

1985   1990   1995   2000

Copyright © McDougal Littell Inc.

Guided Reading

A. Finding Main Ideas As you read the section, fill in the diagram below with key points about the European Union.

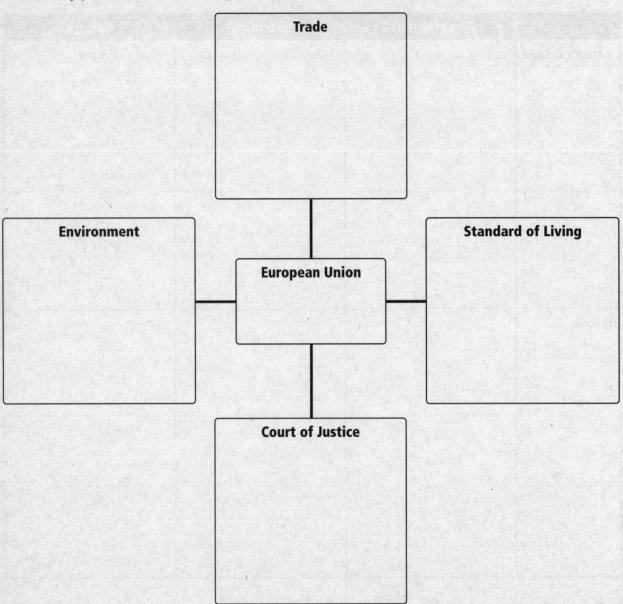

Trade

Environment

European Union

Standard of Living

Court of Justice

B. Drawing Conclusions On the other side of this paper, explain whether or not the European Union will help the countries of Eastern Europe that have yet to join. Give reasons to support your conclusion.

Copyright © McDougal Littell Inc.

CHAPTER 14

Section 1 (pages 379–383)

Guided Reading

A. Categorizing As you read, use the chart below to categorize the information in the section on the United Kingdom.

The United Kingdom		
Government	Economy	Culture

B. Analyzing Causes and Recognizing Effects Use the box labeled *Causes* to explain the events that led up to the signing of the Good Friday Accord. Use the box labeled *Effects* to explain the results of the agreement.

Causes	Good Friday Accord	Effects

Guided Reading

A. Taking Notes As you read this section, take notes on the following topics.

Topics	Notes
Sweden's government	
Sweden's foreign policy	
Sweden's economy	
Power sources	
Acid rain	
Sweden's people	
Recreation	
Writers and filmmakers	

B. Summarizing On the back of this paper, briefly explain Sweden's environmental problems.

Section 3 (pages 390–393)

Guided Reading

A. Finding Main Ideas As you read, take notes to answer these questions about France.

1. What role did Charles de Gaulle play in World War II?
2. How does France's government work?
3. Why did the French government nationalize industry after World War II?
4. Why does France get much of its power from nuclear energy instead of from other sources?
5. What are France's major exports?
6. What role has Paris played in French and European culture?

B. Summarizing On the back of this paper, write what each person contributed to France's culture.

Edouard Manet   **Marcel Proust**   **Albert Camus**   **Simone de Beauvoir**

Guided Reading

A. Finding Main Ideas Fill in the cluster diagrams below with details that relate to the main idea questions.

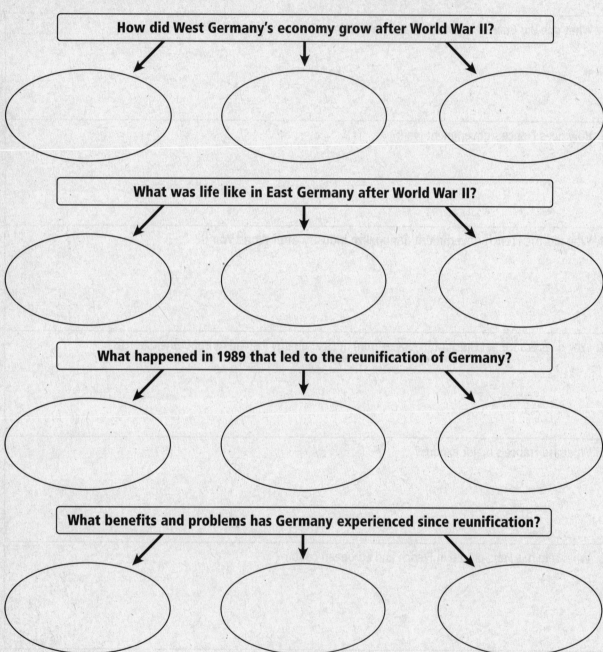

How did West Germany's economy grow after World War II?

What was life like in East Germany after World War II?

What happened in 1989 that led to the reunification of Germany?

What benefits and problems has Germany experienced since reunification?

B. Summarizing On the back of this paper, make a list of the artists described in this section. Next to each name, write what the artist contributed to German culture.

Guided Reading

A. Sequencing Events As you read about the changes in Poland since the end of World War II, fill in the boxes below with descriptions of the events that have occurred.

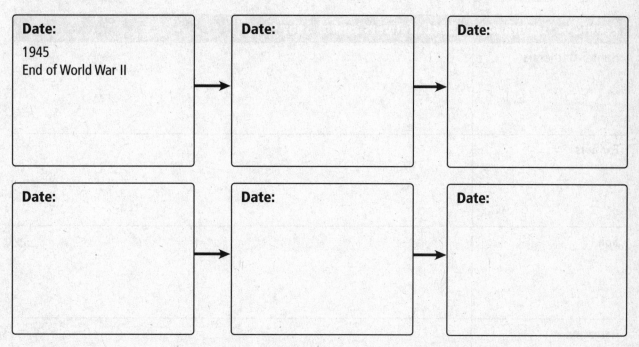

Date:

1945
End of World War II

Date:

Date:

Date:

Date:

Date:

B. Contrasting Use the chart below to list details about the government's role in Polish culture during and after Communist rule.

During Communist Rule	After Communist Rule

Guided Reading

A. Recognizing Effects As you read this section, write notes in the chart below about how the bodies of water (rivers and seas) affect the different people and the geography of North Africa and Southwest Asia.

People or Geography	Effect of Rivers and/or Seas
Hunter-Gatherers	
Farmers	
Soil	
Irrigation	
Trade	
Energy	

B. Summarizing On the back of this paper, write a short paragraph explaining how flooding and rivers are important to farming in North Africa and Southwest Asia.

Copyright © McDougal Littell Inc.

Guided Reading

A. Finding Main Ideas As you read this section, write three details about each of the main ideas in the chart below.

Main Idea	Details
Sumerians built organized city-states.	1. 2. 3.
City-states were centers of religious worship.	1. 2. 3.
Mesopotamia had a class system.	1. 2. 3.
Sumerians developed the first system of writing.	1. 2. 3.

B. Summarizing Imagine that you are a Sumerian scribe. On the back of this paper, write a journal entry about what your schooling is like and what you expect to do with your education once you finish.

Guided Reading

A. Recognizing Important Details As you read the section, answer the
questions about ancient Egyptian life. Write your answers in the chart.

1. In what way was the Nile River unpredictable?	
2. How did ancient Egyptians manage the unpredictable river?	
3. What did ancient Egyptians make using mud from the Nile?	
4. What does a pyramid look like?	
5. What are the pyramids made of?	
6. What two gods were linked to the pharaoh?	
7. Where could common people go to pray and leave offerings to the gods?	

B. Summarizing On the back of this paper, write a paragraph describing the
way average Egyptians buried their dead.

Section 4 (pages 435–439)

Guided Reading

A. Categorizing As you read the section, choose three details from each religion and place them in the proper section of the chart.

Judaism	Christianity	Islam

B. Summarizing Choose one of the religions you learned about in this section, and, using your notes in the chart above, write a short history of the religion on the back of this paper. Describe its history, beliefs, leaders, and any struggles.

Guided Reading

A. Finding Main Ideas As you read the section, fill out the chart below with main ideas and details on the different Muslim empires and groups of people.

Empire	Notes
1. Caliphates	Main Idea: Details:
2. Ottoman Empire	Main Idea: Details:
3. Suleiman I "The Magnificent"	Main Idea: Details:
4. Janissaries	Main Idea: Details:

B. Summarizing On the back of this paper, draw a diagram that shows the five pillars of Islam.

Section 1 (pages 449–453)

Guided Reading

A. Analyzing Causes As you read this section, use the chart below to record the causes of the conflicts in North Africa and Southwest Asia.

Conflict	Causes
Arab-Israeli Wars	1. _____ 2. _____ 3. _____
Conflict between Sunnis and Shi'ites	1. _____
Conflict between Iran and Iraq	1. _____ 2. _____
Conflicts with the Kurds	1. _____
Conflicts between Muslim Iran and other nations	1. _____
Persian Gulf War	1. _____ 2. _____

B. Summarizing On the back of this paper, write a paragraph describing the attempts that have been made to end the Arab-Israeli Wars and bring peace.

Guided Reading

A. Recognizing Important Details As you read the section about the resources and religions of Southwest Asia and North Africa, fill in the cluster diagrams below with names and phrases that relate to the topic in the center oval.

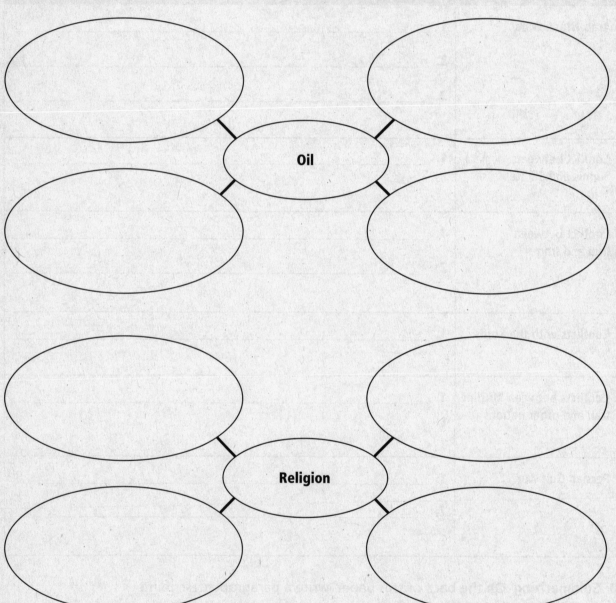

B. Summarizing On the back of this paper, create another cluster diagram with the words "The Roles of Women" in the center oval. Fill in the diagram with names and phrases that relate to the topic in the center.

Copyright © McDougal Littell Inc.

Guided Reading

A. Sequencing Events As you read the section, fill in the time line below with important events about Egypt. Some dates will have more than one event.

1250

_____
_____

—1517
_____
_____

1869 —•
_____
_____

—1922
_____
_____

1952 —•
_____
_____

—1956
_____
_____

1979 —•
_____
_____

2000
_____
_____

B. Summarizing Imagine that you are an Egyptian living in Cairo. Write a paragraph on the back of this paper that describes what life there is like.

CHAPTER 16

Name _____ Date _____

Guided Reading

A. Recognizing Important Details As you read about Israel today, use the following questions to help you record important details from the section.

Who? **1.** Who are the Palestinian Arabs?	
What? **2.** What is Zionism? **3.** What do members of a kibbutz share?	
When? **4.** When were eleven Arabs elected to the Knesset, or Israeli parliament? **5.** When did Israel begin a policy of airlifting groups of Jews?	
Where? **6.** Where did Arab refugees from Israel flee to after the 1948 Arab-Israeli War?	
Why? **7.** Why does Israel have so many Jewish immigrants?	
How? **8.** How does B'Tselem help people?	

B. Summarizing On the back of this paper, write a paragraph describing religion in Israel today.

Section 5 (pages 476–479)

Guided Reading

A. Recognizing Important Details As you read about Turkey, answer the questions about three main topics in the section. Write your answers in the chart.

Mustafa Kemal
1. What was the name of Turkey's first legislature, organized by Kemal?
2. What did Kemal believe about "Western" ways and ideas?
3. What changes did Kemal make to Turkey?
Modernization
4. How did Turkish women benefit from modernization?
Rights and Freedoms
5. How does the Turkish government sometimes limit freedoms?
6. How does the government treat the Kurds?

B. Summarizing On the back of this paper, write a paragraph about modern Turkey's international alliances. Tell what events occurred in 1952 and 1987.

Guided Reading

A. Categorizing As you read the section, fill in the chart below with names and details for each category.

Landforms	Waterways	Climates

B. Summarizing On the back of this paper, make a chart, similar to the one above, listing the renewable and nonrenewable resources of Africa south of the Sahara.

Guided Reading

A. Finding Main Ideas As you read the section, answer the questions about African cultures and empires. Write your answers in the chart below.

Early African Farmers
1. What is the Bantu migration?
2. What did the Bantu do in their new homes?

Trade Networks
3. Why is salt important?
4. What did the people of Southern Africa trade for salt?
5. How did camels help African trade?

Ancient Ghana
6. Why was Ancient Ghana's location important?

The Songhai Empire
7. What Songhai city became the center of Muslim culture?

B. Summarizing On the back of this paper, draw a time line with entries for the main events in the rise and fall of the Mali Empire.

Guided Reading

A. Recognizing Effects As you read the section, fill in the chart with the effects of European colonialism on African life.

Event	Effect
Slave Trade	
Missionaries	
Colonial Rule	

B. Using Maps Using the map on page 510 of your textbook, create a chart listing the European countries that colonized Africa and the colonies each country established. Tell which European nation had the most African colonies in 1912.

Name _____ Date _____

Guided Reading

A. Sequencing Events As you read the section, fill in the events that occurred next to each date in the chart.

Date	Event
1910	
1919	
1920s and 1930s	
1948	
1960	
1963	
1966	
1991	
1994	

B. Summarizing On the back of this paper, write a paragraph explaining why the independence of Nigeria led to riots and violence.

Guided Reading

A. Comparing and Contrasting As you read the section, use the Venn Diagram below to compare and contrast the governments of the Democratic Republic of the Congo and Ghana.

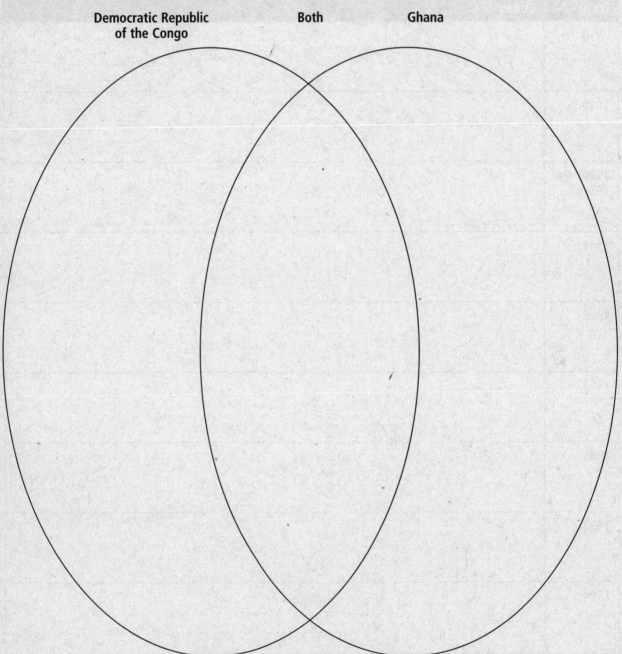

Democratic Republic of the Congo   Both   Ghana

B. Summarizing On the back of this paper, write a paragraph describing what OAU and ECOWAS do to help struggling African nations.

Guided Reading

A. Recognizing Important Details As you read this section, write three details about each of the following main ideas in the chart below.

Main Idea	Details
Most people in Western and Central Africa are farmers.	1. 2. 3.
Although a majority of people are farmers, some have other jobs.	1. 2. 3.
Africa's mineral wealth is sometimes used to help fund wars.	1. 2. 3.

B. Summarizing On the back of this paper, write a paragraph describing family structure, social status, and rites of passage in Western and Central African societies.

Name _____   Date _____

Guided Reading

A. Finding Main Ideas As you read about Nigeria today, use the following
questions to help you record main ideas from the section.

Who? **1.** Who was elected president of Nigeria in 1999? **2.** Who are some of the famous writers of Nigeria?	
What? **3.** What are the three ethnic groups in Nigeria?	
When? **4.** When did Nigeria gain independence from British rule? **5.** When did civil war rage in Nigeria?	
Where? **6.** Where was Queen Amina crowned?	
Why? **7.** Why is more than half of Nigeria's population farmers?	
How? **8.** How did military rule after the civil war affect people's freedoms?	

B. Summarizing On the back of this paper, write a paragraph contrasting
the three ethnic groups in Nigeria: the Yoruba, the Igbo, and the Hausa.

Guided Reading

A. Finding Main Ideas As you read the section, write the main idea about each of the societies of Eastern and Southern Africa in the chart below.

Society	Main Idea
Aksum Empire	
Zimbabwe and Mozambique	
Shona	
Masai	
Zulu	

B. Summarizing On the back of this paper, make a time line of key events in the history of the governments of Somalia and Rwanda.

Guided Reading

A. Categorizing As you read the section, fill in the chart below with names and details about Eastern and Southern African economies and cultures.

Agriculture	Economy	Culture

B. Summarizing Imagine that you are a reporter covering a music concert in Eastern or Southern Africa. On the back of this paper, write a short news article about what you saw and heard. Include details from your chart.

Name _____ Date _____

Guided Reading

A. Sequencing Events As you read the section, fill in events that occurred in South Africa next to each date in the chart.

Date	Event
1652	
1800s	
1850s	
1889–1902	
1896	
1910	
1948	
1950s	
1970s and 1980s	
1985	
1989	
1993	
1999	

B. Summarizing On the back of this paper, write a short paragraph describing economic conditions in South Africa today.

Name _____ Date _____

Guided Reading

A. Recognizing Important Details As you read the section, answer the questions about Kenya. Write your answers in the chart below.

Geography
1. Where does most of Kenya's population live? Why?

History
2. When did Kenya become a British colony?
3. When did Kenya gain its independence?

Government
4. Why did many Kenyans become dissatisfied with the political system in the early 1990s?
5. What did the Kenyans gain through violent demonstrations?

The People of Kenya
6. What are the official languages of Kenya?
7. What are *harambees*?
8. How do most Kenyans earn a living?

B. Summarizing On the back of this paper, write a short paragraph describing Kenya's capital city, Nairobi.

Guided Reading

A. Categorizing As you read the section, write details about each geographic region in the chart below.

Region	Details
The Northern Mountain Rim	
The Northern Plains	
The Deccan Plateau	
Sri Lanka and the Maldives	
Mainland Southeast Asia	
Islands of Southeast Asia	

B. Summarizing On the back of this paper, write a paragraph that describes the climates of South Asia and Southeast Asia.

Guided Reading

A. Recognizing Effects As you read the section, fill in the chart below with the effects of each civilization or religion on the culture of India.

Civilization or Religion	Effects
Aryans, 1700 B.C.	
Hinduism	
Mauryan Empire, 324–185 B.C.	
Gupta Dynasty, A.D. 320–500	

B. Summarizing On the back of this paper, write a paragraph explaining the Hindu caste system.

Guided Reading

A. Finding Main Ideas As you read about the culture of ancient Southeast Asia, answer the following questions to help you record main ideas from the section.

Who? **1.** Who is the founder of Buddhism?	
What? **2.** What important skills were developed in ancient Southeast Asia? **3.** What are some of the trade goods of Southeast Asia?	
When? **4.** When was the Buddhist temple called Borobudur built? **5.** When did king Anawrahta establish a strong Buddhist kingdom?	
Where? **6.** Where was the Khmer kingdom?	
Why? **7.** Why did the Khmer lose power?	
How? **8.** How did the founder of Buddhism obtain enlightenment?	

B. Summarizing On the back of this paper, explain the Four Noble Truths that are the basic teachings of Buddhism.

Guided Reading

A. Sequencing Events As you read the section, fill in the time line below with important events in the history of India and its neighbors.

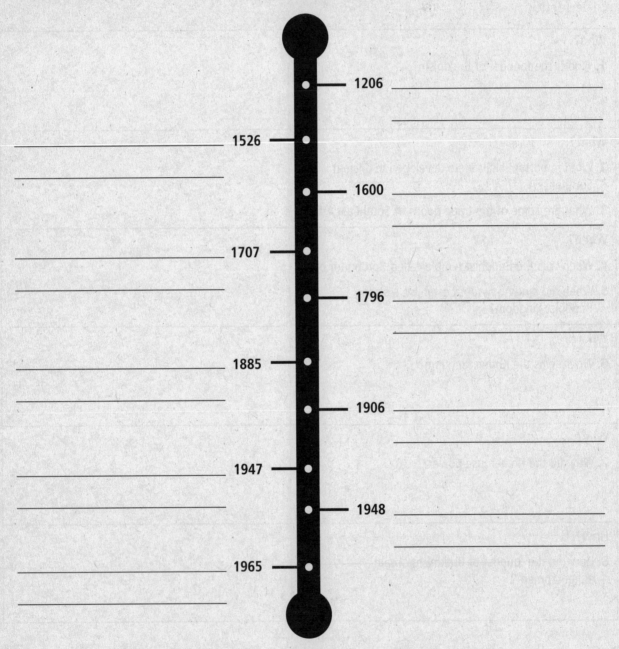

1206 _____
_____

1526 _____

1600 _____
_____

1707 _____

1796 _____
_____

1885 _____

1906 _____
_____

1947 _____

1948 _____
_____

1965 _____

B. Summarizing On the back of this paper, write a short paragraph describing the beliefs and actions of Mohandas Gandhi.

Section 2 (pages 615–619)

Guided Reading

A. Categorizing As you read the section, fill in events and important details about the governments of South Asia.

Governments	Details
Afghanistan	
Bangladesh	
Bhutan	
The Maldives	
Nepal	
Pakistan	
Sri Lanka	

B. Summarizing On the back of this paper, create and fill in a two-column chart, similar to the one above, for India's government. Column headings should be *India's Government* and *Details.* For the row headings, use the following four categories: *Democracy, Caste System, Women,* and *Village Government.*

Guided Reading

A. Categorizing As you read the section, fill in events and important details about the economies of South Asia.

Economies	Details
Afghanistan	
Bangladesh	
Bhutan and Nepal	
The Maldives	
Pakistan	
Sri Lanka	
India	

B. Summarizing On the back of this paper, write a short paragraph describing the Green Revolution.

Guided Reading

A. Finding Main Ideas As you read the section, answer the questions about India's culture. Write your answers in the chart.

The Taj Mahal
1. What does the Taj Mahal symbolize in India today?

India and the Arts
2. What are two great works of Indian literature?
3. Where is music played in India?

Languages
4. How many official languages are there in India?
5. What two language families do most Indian languages come from?

Religion
6. To what religion do most Indians belong?

Family
7. What must a bride's parents provide to her new husband and his family?

B. Summarizing On the back of this paper, write a short paragraph describing the kinds of foods in a typical Indian meal.

CHAPTER 21 **Section 5** (pages 631–635)

Guided Reading

A. Recognizing Important Details As you read about Pakistan, answer the following questions to help you record important details from the section.

Who? **1.** Who was Governor-General Mohammed Ali Jinnah?	
What? **2.** What are the four provinces of Pakistan? **3.** What are the three main languages of Pakistan?	
When? **4.** When did Pakistan gain its independence? **5.** When did Pakistan finish building the Mangla Dam?	
Where? **6.** Where is the Tarbela Dam located?	
Why? **7.** Why did relations between Pakistan and India grow tense in 1998?	
How? **8.** How did the British influence Pakistan when they ruled the country?	

B. Summarizing On the back of this paper, write a paragraph describing the geography of the provinces of Pakistan.

Guided Reading

A. Recognizing Important Details As you read this section, write three details about each of the main ideas in the chart below.

Main Idea	Details
India and China had influence on Southeast Asia.	1. 2. 3.
Trade with other parts of the world brought Christianity and Islam to Southeast Asia.	1. 2. 3.
European colonization brought new goods to Southeast Asia.	1. 2. 3.
After gaining independence, many nations in Southeast Asia found themselves in political turmoil.	1. 2. 3.

B. Summarizing On the back of this paper, write a paragraph describing what mandalas are and how they were constructed in Southeast Asia.

Guided Reading

A. Categorizing As you read this section, fill in the chart with names and details about the culture of Southeast Asia for each category.

Culture of Southeast Asia	
Languages	
Religions	
Architecture	
Dance	
Weaving	

B. Summarizing On the back of this paper, make a chart similar to the one above to describe the agricultural economy of Southeast Asia. Use the following three categories: *Small Farms, Factories,* and *Singapore.*

Guided Reading

A. Finding Main Ideas As you read the section, answer the questions about Vietnam. Write your answers in the chart below.

A History of Struggle
1. During China's rule over Vietnam, how did China help Vietnam advance?
2. Why did Napoleon III invade Vietnam?

War
3. Who became the leader of Vietnam's independence movement?
4. What did the agreement in 1954 do to Vietnam?
5. Why did the United States get involved in the conflict in Vietnam?

Vietnam Today
6. How many political parties are there in Vietnam?
7. How did the policy of *doi moi* help the economy of Vietnam?

B. Summarizing On the back of this paper, write a short article about life in Vietnam today. Include details about where people live and what important holiday is celebrated.

Name _____ Date _____

Guided Reading

A. Categorizing As you read the section, write details about the geography of China, Japan, Korea, and Australia.

China	Mountains: Rivers: Deserts:
Japan	Mountains and Volcanoes: Earthquakes: Climate:
The Koreas	Rivers: Climate:
Australia	Flat and Dry: Great Barrier Reef:

B. Summarize On the back of this paper, list three details about the geography of the Koreas and three details about the geography of New Zealand and the Pacific Islands.

Guided Reading

A. Recognizing Effects As you read the section on Ancient China, fill in the chart to show how each achievement affected the people, culture, or economy of China.

Achievement	Effects
Silk	
The Silk Road	
Porcelain	
Writing	
The Great Builders	

B. Summarize On the back of this paper, create a diagram showing the three religions mentioned in this section and the main ideas of each one.

Guided Reading

A. Recognizing Important Details As you read the section, answer the questions about Ancient Japan. Write your answers in the chart below.

Early Japan
1. What religion did the early Japanese practice? What does its name mean?
2. How were the early Japanese kingdoms organized?

Outside Influence
3. What knowledge did the Japanese gain from Koreans?
4. What did the Japanese gain from an exchange with China?
5. What was the name of the world's first novel?
6. Which branch of Buddhism was the most influential in Japan?

Feudal Japan
7. What was the name of the new kind of warrior government in Japan in 1192?
8. How did Tokugawa Ieyasu close the door to Japan?

B. Summarizing On the back of this paper, write a short description of a samurai. Explain what his purpose was and what his armor was like.

Guided Reading

A. Sequencing Events As you read the section, fill in the time line below with important events in China.

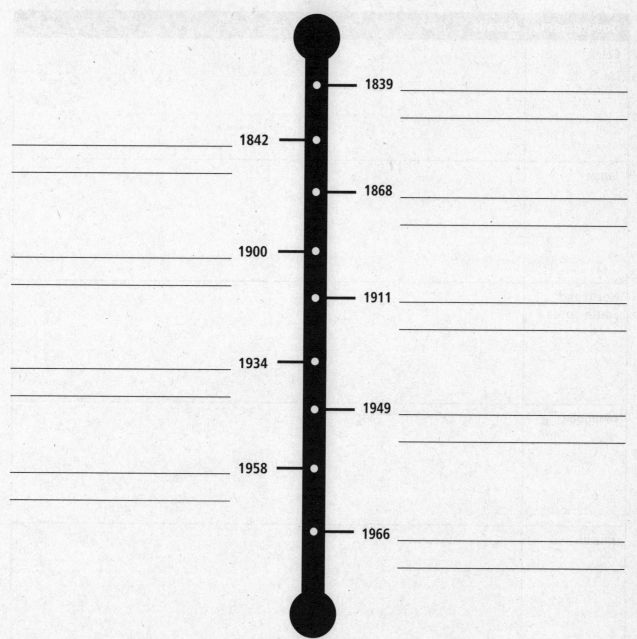

1839 _____

1842 _____

1868 _____

1900 _____

1911 _____

1934 _____

1949 _____

1958 _____

1966 _____

B. Summarizing Imagine you are a person living in China during the rule of Mao Zedong. Write a short journal entry describing the Great Leap Forward and the Cultural Revolution.

Guided Reading

A. Categorizing As you read the section, fill in events and important details about the governments of countries in East Asia.

Governments	Details
China	
Japan	
North and South Korea	
Mongolia	
Taiwan	

B. Summarizing On the back of this paper, write a paragraph describing the events that occurred in Tiananmen Square in 1989.

Guided Reading

A. Categorizing As you read the section, fill in events and important details about the economies of countries in East Asia.

Economies	Details
Taiwan	
North Korea	
South Korea	
Japan	

B. Summarizing On the back of this paper, write a paragraph describing the economy of China. Include information about China's industry and farming.

Guided Reading

A. Finding Main Ideas As you read the section, answer these questions about the cultures of East Asia.

Cultural Exchange
1. Where did most shared aspects of East Asian culture originate?
2. What religions are practiced throughout East Asia today?
Arts
3. What kinds of instruments are played in China?
4. What do Japanese artists consider important in their artwork?
Culture and Communism
5. What happened to culture during the Cultural Revolution in China?
The Chinese People
6. To what ethnic group do most people in China belong?

B. Summarizing On the back of this paper, write a paragraph describing some of the changes in Chinese family structure.

Guided Reading

A. Recognizing Important Details As you read about modern Japan, use the following questions to help you record important details from the section.

Who? **1.** Who was Matthew C. Perry?	
What? **2.** What happened during the Meiji Restoration? **3.** What aspects of Japanese culture have become popular in the United States?	
When? **4.** When did Japan invade China? **5.** When did Japan bomb the U.S. naval base at Pearl Harbor?	
Where? **6.** Where in Japan did the United States drop two atomic bombs?	
Why? **7.** Why is most of Japan's population homogeneous?	
How? **8.** What fraction of Japanese women hold jobs?	

B. Summarizing On the back of this paper, write a paragraph describing the social customs of Japanese people.

Guided Reading

A. Recognizing Important Details As you read this section, write two or three details about each of the main ideas in the chart below.

Main Idea	Details
Geography influenced which islands people settled.	1. 2.
European exploration in the Pacific had negative effects on the islanders.	1. 2. 3.
European settlement had negative effects on the Aborigines of Australia.	1. 2. 3.

B. Summarizing On the back of this paper, create a chart that shows characteristics of the governments of Australia, New Zealand, and Oceania.

Guided Reading

A. Categorizing As you read the section, fill in the cluster diagrams with information about the economy and culture of **(1)** Australia and New Zealand and **(2)** Oceania. For each area, fill in two of the ovals with information about the economy and two with information about culture.

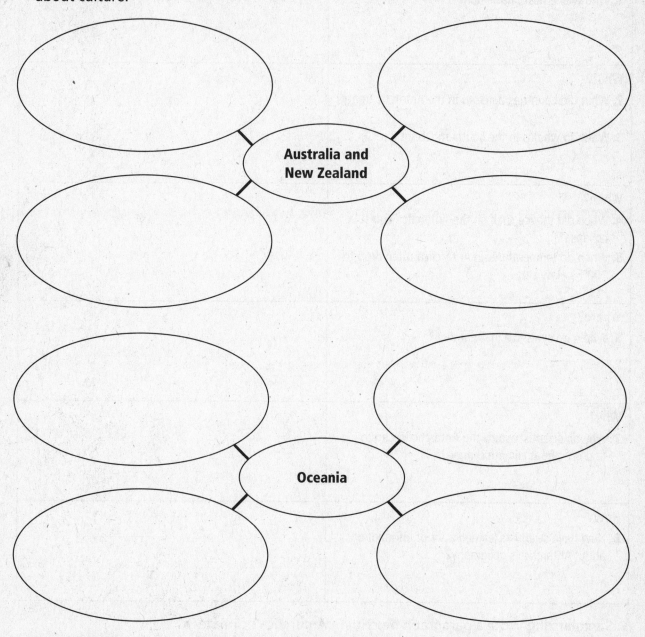

Australia and New Zealand

Oceania

B. Summarizing On the back of this paper, explain why Charlie Perkins is important.

Guided Reading

A. Recognizing Important Details As you read about Antarctica, use the
   following questions to help you record important details from the section.

Who? **1.** Who was Ernest Shackleton?	
What? **2.** What did countries agree to in the Antarctic Treaty? **3.** What do whales in the Southern Ocean eat?	
When? **4.** When did the ice shelf on the Antarctic Peninsula collapse? **5.** When do temperatures in Antarctica often drop to 100°F below zero?	
Where? **6.** Where do seals live in Antarctica?	
Why? **7.** Why do scientists study the Antarctic icecap to find out about climate change?	
How? **8.** How have scientists learned a lot of information about Antarctica's geography?	

B. Summarizing Write a paragraph describing Antarctica's climate.